For my sister Teresa

Praise for
EASTER and THE FIRST CHRISTMAS
by Jan Pieńkowski

★ "Dazzling beauty and poignant emotion suffuse these illustrations,
which give an intensely personal interpretation of the King James
Version of the Easter gospels."
—*School Library Journal*, Starred

"This is a masterful visual ode to a biblical story,
and will give readers of any age a cornucopia of images
to pore over and think about."
—*Publishers Weekly*

★ "A memorable, dramatic, reverent presentation."
—*Kirkus Reviews*, Starred

"Visual splendor." —*Winston-Salem Journal*

"Breathtaking." —*San Francisco Chronicle*

"The glory of the verse is matched by
the exquisite illustrations."
—*The Baltimore Sun*

"Spectacular!" —*Chicago Sun-Times*

Easter

The King James Version
with pictures
by

Jan Pieńkowski

ALFRED A. KNOPF 🐎 NEW YORK

IN THE REIGN of Tiberius Caesar, Pontius
Pilate being governor of Judaea, many
went up to Jerusalem for the Passover. And
Jesus took the twelve disciples and came to Bethany where
Lazarus was whom he raised from the dead. There they made
him a supper, and Martha served.

Then took Mary a pound of ointment of spikenard, very
costly, and anointed the feet of Jesus, and wiped his feet
with her hair.

Then saith one of his disciples, Judas Iscariot, Why was not this ointment sold for three hundred pence, and given to the poor? Then said Jesus, Let her alone: against the day of my burying hath she done this.

Then Judas went to the chief priests, and said, What will ye give me and I will deliver him to you? And they promised to give him thirty pieces of silver.

And from that time he sought opportunity to betray him.

ON THE NEXT DAY much people that were come to the feast, when they heard that Jesus was coming to Jerusalem, spread their garments in the way: and others cut down branches off the trees, and strawed them in the way.

And they that went before, and they that followed, cried, saying Hosanna! Blessed is he that cometh in the name of the Lord! Hosanna in the highest!

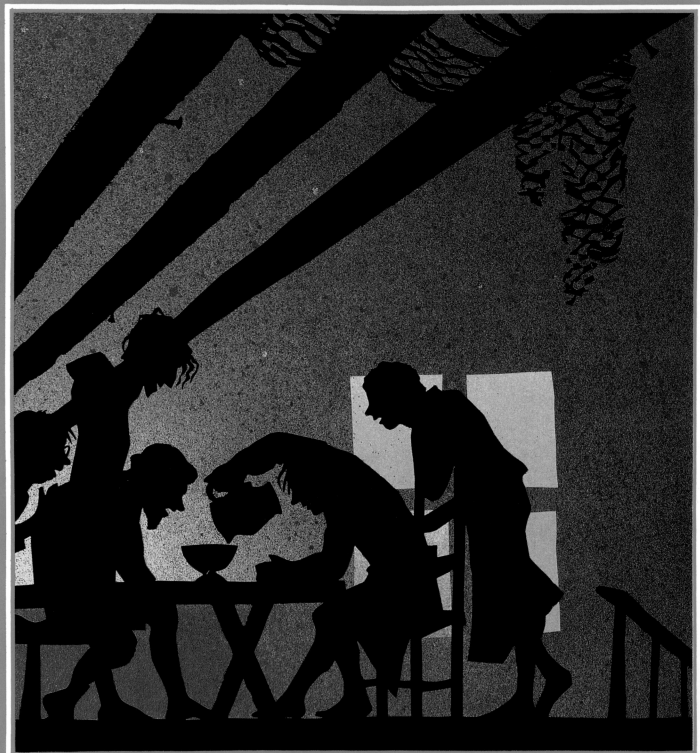

Then came the day of the feast of unleavened bread and the disciples made ready the Passover.

Now when the even was come, he sat down with the twelve.

And as they were eating, Jesus took bread, and gave thanks and brake it, and gave unto them, saying, This is my body which is given for you: this do in remembrance of me.

Likewise also the cup after supper, saying, This cup is my blood, which is shed for you.

HE LAID ASIDE his garments and took a towel, and he poureth water into a basin, and began to wash the disciples' feet, and to wipe them with the towel.

After he had washed their feet, he said to them, Ye call me Master and Lord for so I am. If I then, your Lord and Master, have washed your feet; ye also ought to wash one another's feet.

And Jesus said, One of you shall betray me.
And they began to be sorrowful, and to say to him
one by one, Is it I? and another said, Is it I?
Then Judas said, Master, is it I?
He said unto him, Thou hast said.
    He then went immediately out:
and it was night.

THEREFORE, WHEN he was gone out,
    Jesus said, Little children, yet a little while
    I am with you.
Whither I go, ye cannot come.

    A new commandment I give unto you, That ye love one
another as I have loved you.

Peter said, Lord, whither goest thou? Jesus answered, Whither I go, thou canst not follow me now; but thou shalt follow me afterwards.

Peter said, Lord, why cannot I follow thee now? I will lay down my life for thy sake. Jesus said, I tell thee Peter, this night, before the cock crow, thou shalt deny me thrice.

AND WHEN they had sung an hymn, they went out into the Mount of Olives. And he was withdrawn from them about a stone's cast, and kneeled down, and prayed, Father, all things are possible unto thee; take away this cup from me; nevertheless not my will, but thine, be done.

And he cometh to the disciples and findeth them asleep, and saith unto Peter, What, could ye not watch with me one hour?

He went away again the second time and prayed. And being in an agony he prayed more earnestly: and his sweat was as it were great drops of blood falling down to the ground. And he came and found them asleep again: for their eyes were heavy.

And he cometh the third time, and saith to them, Why sleep ye? Rise up, let us go; lo, he that betrayeth me is at hand.

And while he yet spake, Judas came, and with him a great multitude with swords and staves, from the chief priests and leaders of the people.

He had given them a sign, saying, Whomsoever I shall kiss, that same is he: hold him fast. And forthwith he came to Jesus and said, Hail, master; and kissed him.

But Jesus said to him, Judas, betrayest thou the Son of man with a kiss?

THEN PETER having a sword drew it, and smote the high priest's servant, and cut off his right ear. Then said Jesus, Put up thy sword; for all they that take the sword shall perish with the sword. And he touched his ear, and healed him.

Then all the disciples forsook him, and fled.

They led Jesus away into the high priest's house. And Peter followed afar off and sat with the servants, and warmed himself at the fire.

But a certain maid earnestly looked upon him and said, Thou also wast with Jesus. And he denied, saying, Woman, I know him not.

After a little while another saw him, and said, Surely, thou also art one of them. And Peter said, Man, I am not.

And about one hour after one of the servants, being his kinsman whose ear Peter cut off, saith, Did not I see thee with him? And Peter said, Man, I know not what thou sayest.

And immediately the cock crew. And the Lord turned, and looked upon Peter.

And Peter went out, and wept bitterly.

AND THE HIGH PRIEST arose, and said, Tell us whether thou be the Christ, the Son of God. And Jesus said, I am. Then the high priest rent his clothes, saying, Behold, now ye have heard his blasphemy, what think ye? They answered, He is guilty of death.

When morning was come, they led him away to Pontius Pilate.

Then Judas repented, and brought again the thirty pieces of silver to the chief priests and elders, saying, I have betrayed the innocent blood. And they said, What is that to us? see thou to that. And he cast down the pieces of silver and departed, and went and hanged himself.

ESUS STOOD before the governor: and the governor asked him, Art thou the King of the Jews? And Jesus said, Thou sayest it.

Pilate went out unto the Jews, and saith to them, I find in him no fault at all. But ye have a custom, that I should release unto you one at the Passover: Will ye therefore that I release unto you the King of the Jews?

Then cried they all, Not this man but Barabbas.

Now Barabbas was a robber.

And Pilate said again to them, What will ye then that I shall do unto him whom ye call the King of the Jews? And they cried out, Crucify him. Then Pilate said, Why, what evil hath he done? And they cried out the more exceedingly, Crucify him.

When Pilate saw that he could prevail nothing, he took
water, and washed his hands before the multitude, saying,
I am innocent of the blood of this just person. Then released
he Barabbas unto them: and when he had scourged Jesus,
he delivered him to be crucified.

THE SOLDIERS platted a crown of thorns,
and put it on his head, and they put on him
a purple robe. And they bowed the knee before
him saying, Hail, King of the Jews! And they smote him with
their hands.

After they had mocked him they took the robe off from him
and led him away to crucify him.

AS THEY LED him away, they laid hold upon one Simon, a Cyrenian, coming out of the country, and on him they laid the cross, that he might bear it after Jesus.

And there followed him a great company of people and of women, which bewailed and lamented him.

And when they were come to the place which is called Calvary, there they crucified him, and with him two thieves; the one on his right hand, and the other on his left.

Then said Jesus, Father, forgive them: for they know not what they do.

And it was the third hour.

One of the thieves which were crucified with him railed on him, saying, If thou be Christ, save thyself and us. But the other rebuked him, saying, Dost not thou fear God? For we receive the due reward of our deeds: but this man hath done nothing amiss. And he said to Jesus, Lord, remember me when thou comest into thy kingdom.

And Jesus said to him, Today shalt thou be with me in paradise.

NOW THERE STOOD by the cross of Jesus his mother, and his mother's sister, and Mary Magdalene. When Jesus saw his mother and the disciple whom he loved, he saith to his mother, Woman, behold thy son! Then saith he to the disciple, Behold thy mother!

And from that hour that disciple took her unto his own home.

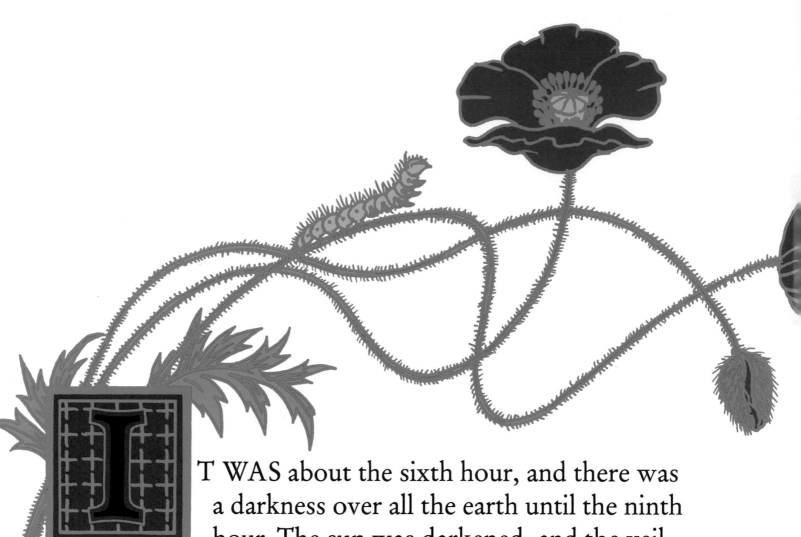

IT WAS about the sixth hour, and there was a darkness over all the earth until the ninth hour. The sun was darkened, and the veil of the temple was rent in twain from the top to the bottom; and the earth did quake, and the rocks rent.

And when Jesus had cried with a loud voice, he said, Father, into thy hands I commend my spirit: and having said thus, he gave up the ghost.

Now when the centurion, and they that were with him, saw the earthquake, they feared greatly, saying, Truly this was the Son of God.

When the even was come, there came a rich man of Arimathaea, named Joseph, who also was Jesus' disciple.

He went boldly to Pilate, and begged the body of Jesus. Then Pilate commanded the body to be delivered.

AND WHEN JOSEPH had taken the body, he wrapped it in a clean linen cloth with spices, myrrh, and aloes, and laid it in his own new tomb which he had hewn out in the rock.

And he rolled a great stone to the door of the sepulcher, and departed.

A S IT BEGAN to dawn came Mary Magdalene and found the stone rolled away. Then she runneth to Peter, and to the other disciple, and saith, They have taken away the Lord. So they ran to the sepulcher, and saw, and believed.

Then the disciples went away to their home, but Mary stood at the sepulcher weeping, and as she wept she saw two angels sitting where the body of Jesus had lain. And they say,

Woman, why weepest thou? She saith, Because they have
taken away my Lord, and I know not where they have laid
him. And she turned and saw Jesus standing, and knew not
that it was Jesus.

Jesus saith, Woman, why weepest thou? whom seekest thou?
She, supposing him to be the gardener, saith, Sir, if thou
have borne him hence, tell me where thou hast laid him.

Jesus saith unto her, Mary. She turned and saith unto him,
Rabboni; which is to say Master.

Mary Magdalene came and told the disciples.

THE SAME EVENING, when the disciples were assembled came Jesus and stood in the midst, and saith, Peace be unto you. Then were the disciples glad, when they saw the Lord.

But Thomas, one of the twelve, was not with them when Jesus came. The other disciples therefore said to him, We have seen the Lord. But he said to them, Except I see in his hands the print of the nails, and put my finger into the print of the nails, I will not believe.

And after eight days again his disciples were within, and Thomas with them. Then came Jesus, the doors being shut, and stood in the midst, and said to Thomas, Reach hither thy finger, and behold my hands; and be not faithless, but believing. And Thomas answered and said unto him, My Lord and my God.

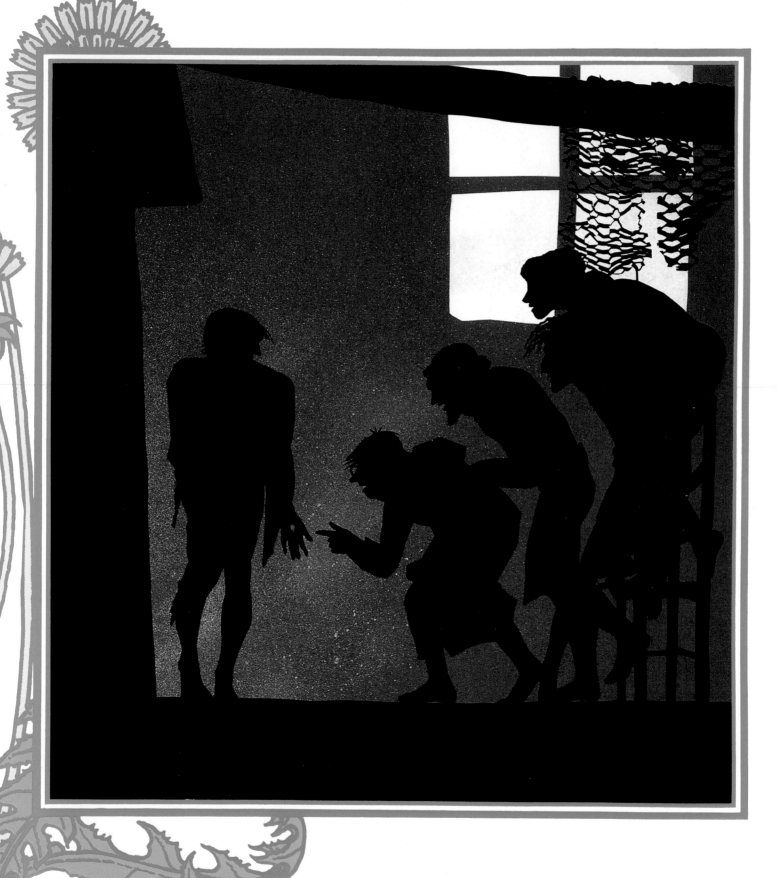

Jesus saith to Thomas, Because thou hast seen me, thou hast believed; blessed are they that have not seen, and yet have believed.

GO YE THEREFORE, and teach all nations, baptizing them in the name of the Father, and of the Son, and of the Holy Ghost. And lo, I am with you always, even unto the end of the world.

THIS IS A BORZOI BOOK PUBLISHED BY ALFRED A. KNOPF

The following are extracts from the Authorized King James Version of the Bible, which is Crown Copyright in England:
Matthew 26:14–17, 19, 20, 25–6, 34, 40, 42–3, 47–9, 52, 56, 62–3, 65–6, 73; 27:1–5, 11, 24, 26, 29, 31, 44, 51,
54, 57–60; 28:1, 19–20
Mark 11:8–10; 14:11, 18–19, 26, 36, 41–2, 44, 53–4, 62, 67; 15:2, 12–14, 25, 27, 43; 16:5
Luke 3:1; 22:7, 19–20, 34, 41–2, 44, 46, 48, 51, 54–60; 23:26–7, 33–4, 39–46, 55–6; 24:2
John 11:55; 12:1–5, 7, 12; 13:4–5, 12–14, 30, 34, 36–7; 18:10, 26, 38–40; 19:2–3, 25–7, 39; 20:2, 4, 8, 10–16, 18–20, 24–29

The illustrator would like to thank the following for their help: Douglas Martin, Hilary Saunders, and Jane Walmsley.

Cover art and interior illustrations copyright © 1989 by Jan Pieńkowski

All rights reserved. Published in the United States by Alfred A. Knopf, an imprint of Random House Children's Books,
a division of Random House LLC, a Penguin Random House Company, New York. Originally published in hardcover in
Great Britain by William Heinemann Ltd., London, and simultaneously published in hardcover in the United States by
Alfred A. Knopf, an imprint of Random House Children's Books, New York, in 1989.

Knopf, Borzoi Books, and the colophon are registered trademarks of Random House LLC.

Visit us on the Web! randomhouse.com/kids

Educators and librarians, for a variety of teaching tools, visit us at
RHTeachersLibrarians.com

Library of Congress Cataloging-in-Publication Data is available upon request.
ISBN 978-0-385-39277-8 (trade) — ISBN 978-0-385-39278-5 (ebook)

MANUFACTURED IN CHINA
February 2015
10 9 8 7 6 5 4 3 2 1

Random House Children's Books supports the First Amendment and celebrates the right to read.